Charles Kadima

ANGELINA

Charles Kadima

ANGELINA

Clipped at Birth

JustFiction Edition

Imprint
Any brand names and product names mentioned in this book are subject to trademark, brand or patent protection and are trademarks or registered trademarks of their respective holders. The use of brand names, product names, common names, trade names, product descriptions etc. even without a particular marking in this work is in no way to be construed to mean that such names may be regarded as unrestricted in respect of trademark and brand protection legislation and could thus be used by anyone.

Cover image: www.ingimage.com

Publisher:
JustFiction! Edition
is a trademark of
Dodo Books Indian Ocean Ltd., member of the OmniScriptum S.R.L Publishing group
str. A.Russo 15, of. 61, Chisinau-2068, Republic of Moldova Europe
Printed at: see last page
ISBN: 978-613-7-38498-5

ANGELINA

(Clipped at Birth)

Charles Manda Kadima.

In loving memories of my son Prince.

<u>**Preface.**</u>

"....It became a scar that could not heal,
a vacuum that no human could fill,
the sky that do not touch the ground,
a square that is not round,
the dead that do not produce a sound,
and the lost in my life that were never to be found..."

Introduction.

Every person is infinitely vaster in scope than what appears to the naked eyes. For that reason, to have a great sense of who we are and where we are heading to, we have to employ a point of view that is penetrating and catches like radar, to notice the images that might pass unnoticed; one such image of a parent in the lives of their children; parents are an invisible world that strongly affects the visible worlds of their children. Parents bring the past flavors of life, hidden family traditions, on to the table of the children's lives. A child who lacks this figure is permanently divided and alienated from his physical world.

Every single child that is born is a gift from God. That child must be allowed to grow and fulfil its purpose on earth and has a right to an inclusive parenting from both its biological parents and the society at large. For it takes a village to raise a child. For that reason, any decision to have or not have a child should be made before conception because after; then it is to be given a chance to see the world. Live in a home full of love so that the child can become that which God created it to be. No child is a mistake!

Read this story. It is timely, intuitive and educative.

Chapter 1.

I fell in love with my brother. My name is Angelina Achieng Awiti. This is how it all started......

On the 7th day of the 7th month of the year 1989, my good mother decided to go visit her maternal home. Mama had no idea what was waiting for her on the road... If only she knew; if only she had a clue; maybe things could have been different....

The two villages of Mango: where she came from and Ndula: where she got married to, stood side by side, eye to eye like two heavy weight champions who were ready to tare each other down at the strike of a bell.

Legend has it that, these villages came from Omengo and Andola who were twin brothers. They were "Inda Simba" to Mama Mugenya who came with them when she was getting married to Olwanda, her husband.

From childhood to adulthood, a bitter rivalry had grew between the two brothers making it difficult for them to see eye to eye. They never agreed on anything. Any form of unfair treatment to either from the parents, was used as a scapegoat to fight and prove supremacy. And so to ensure that the two were apart, elders of the land advised their father to give them lands that were separated by the long snaking river "Bulamu", thus the birth of the two communities.

"Bulamu" river served not only as a source of life but also as a uniting factor for the two warring communities. Elders from the two villages converged there once a month to discuss issues affecting the land. The meetings were predicated by a series of entertainments that included bull fighting contests:

'Okwiri'; the most feared and strongest bull from Mango Village could face 'Isuna' from Ndula; that was never to be underestimated by its size: for it earned the name mosquito from its small body but big sharp horns that could tare through the flesh of any bull that dared to face it in such contests. Villagers from the two communities could stand on both sides of the river and cheer the bulls from either sides. To them, this was a symbol of the long innate battle that raged between the two communities.

Early in the morning, before smoke could be seen emerging from the round thatched houses all over the two villages, you would see young girls balancing water pots on their heads and swinging their waists from this source of water. Young boys on the other hand could whistle and put up a mock fight just to entertain and try to beguile and woo these girls, or to announce their presence.

The girls who were ready for betrothal used this opportunity to show how all-rounded they were; for only lazy girls clocked twenty years still in their father's houses, they were referred to as, 'efikwakwata' empty boxes, and were to be avoided by men like a plague. The two communities intermarried and this sealed a friendship that was to be enjoyed "efisoni nefisoni". Time went by and the two villages grew into small modern towns; the current Mango and Ndula sub-counties of Mulembe County.

That was then and how Amos Kwale; my father met Sharon Adele Kwale; my good mother.

My father was not just an ordinary village lad; he was a striking handsome; polished eloquent and a well groomed young man in his early twenties. He was always officially dressed and his afro hair was well camped. A real gem to die for at that age in time. Apart from his physical looks, he was also very ambitious and smart. While most of his mates built round thatched houses as their 'tsisimba', my father shocked everyone by building a two bedroom house as his first home; to him, standards were not his children but he had vowed to raise them in all spheres of his life.

By the time he was meeting my mother, he had done well for himself as far as his career and education were concerned. He had a higher diploma in Journalism and went further to establish 'Golden Pen', a top publishing house that was loved and hated in equal measure at the heart of Mulembe County.

The Pen ran a weekly paper which covered all the town's gossip; from who got married, who died, and local sports. My father loved obituaries; he made it fun to die in the Mulembe; he could seize the opportunity and skilfully articulate these messages in away that people could look forward to the next death so that they can read the next issue; most importantly if it was a VIP who had passed on or one of their close family members.

This paper made him famous. Many wanted if not a piece of him, then a piece of his writings. People referred to him as 'Olwino', and indeed he left positive mark in the hearts of many, but his progeny....

So when he approached my mother, she already knew who he was; she was his number one reader. Deep in her heart she knew she had gotten the best she ever wanted in a man; a provider, protector and a man to precede her in all spheres of life. But the two were world apart as far as education was concerned. Mama had only managed to go up to grade five. Those days, parents paid little attention to the education of girls. To them, girls were someone else's property, whose primary goal was to get married to a wealthy man and bare children. The only reason why they were protected was because they were a symbol of family wealth and prosperity.

But Mama caught my father's attention by her unmatched beauty. Unusual as it sounded those days, their relationship started with love; a love that was so kind and true. He saw his entire future in her brown eyes. Her lilting voice was so refreshing that he could listen to her all day long. My mother's beauty in his eyes was a combination of the ancient Queen Cleopatra and Venus the goddess of beauty; her smile was one to die for and all these were well complimented by her beautiful curves and edges which made eight his favourite number; this inspiring their marriage date of August 8th 1970 and also the day mama signed her death certificate.......

On this fateful day, mama really wanted to talk to grandma; the whole day, she felt restless; in fact, the main reason she wanted to talk to her mother was about the dream she had had the previous night.

In her dream, she was in the middle of a desert. Mama was alone; and it was dark. She needed water so badly but as it seemed, there was no source of water around and if it were, she was too exhausted to locate it. Mama tried to move but she could not. All over sudden, the Sky opened and it started to rain; the rain was only covering one square meter; leaving the other parts of the whole desert dry. She smiled and gathered the last strength she had to move where it was raining to quench her thirst. No sooner had she lifted her foot than the rains stopped, and a beam of light shone from the sky again pointing where the rain was falling; the light was actually from the sun but only focused at that point leaving total darkness on other areas around. "So strange that the sun would shine at night!" She spoke to herself moving at that area. Something again caught her attention. This time, it was a beautiful girl resembling an Angel standing next to her; She moved closer and was amazed to notice that the Angel's wings had actually collected water enough to quench her thirst. But before she could start to drink, she heard someone calling from far, it was my father asking for his socks. The calling cut off the dream; but it did not stop her from introspecting about what it was all about. But who else to interpret it other than grandma?

Mama was expectant; she had carried me in her womb for nine months. This gave her joy and she did it with love that she even forgot I needed to come out. She had been married to my dad for three decades now, all these years, mama had never been blessed with the fruit of the womb. This became a thorn on the foot of my parent's marriage. As it was expected, in those days; infertility was viewed as a women problem; Mama was labelled the problem, in fact, my dad had gone fourth to prove that he was not the problem by siring twenty two daughters and one son outside wedlock; each with their mother.

To a man, this was allowed and it boosted their egos high making their counterparts feel unworthy. But my father was not happy. He hated the fact that almost all his children were girls; in fact, non of the children was from his matrimonial tie. People started to talk, and much as the society had evolved and embraced modernity, the issue of a man not being able to sire male children was consequential: for the man had no say where real men were, and was viewed as 'Omutofu'; for he could not stand a war. Male children were like warriors in a homestead; the were the shield and arrow in a man's hand in times of war. They were also viewed as the banks that protected, channelled and controlled the flow of the family river. Without them, these rivers go astray. That was the situation in Kwale's home.

He was forced to look for plan 'B', maybe to massage his ego, and this hurt my mother and broke her heart to pieces. She felt betrayed by the man who had swept her off her feet. The love that she had for him still remained but he stopped caring. Mama did not give up her marriage just like that. She exercised fidelity to the 'till death do us part' vow that she had committed thirty years then at the alter: she remained loyal and hopeful like the biblical Sarah that one day she will carry a fruit of her own womb for Abraham her husband.

My father was very happy when he learned that Mama was pregnant and all the nine months that mama carried me, dad was supportive. He had vowed to change and become true to his calling as a husband as it was before. He had even made a bed for me and painted my room blue; this also worried my mother. He wanted this so badly and never hid it from mama. To him, girls were no longer welcomed. He was expecting a stone for his sling from his lawfully married wife. This would cement their relationship and maybe be the glue needed to bind the broken ties.

Mama had forgotten and it seemed like if it were in her powers, she would have loved to keep me inside for good; maybe because she foresaw and knew what the world had in store for me, she knew if I am left in her womb, she would care and keep me protected closer to her heart. She just switched off from the biological calendar and chose to love every minute she had me kicking her stomach. But since it was not in her powers to decide when I'll come; these powers only God, giver of life has; her water broke just near her mother's gate; and there I was, ready to run my race!

The women of yesterday were strong: maybe because of the lifestyle they led plus the foods they ate. The modern cesarean or prenatal clinics were unheard of. A local midwife was enough to help them deliver and others even did it on their own; some did not know the dangers they exposed the infants and even themselves by not going for clinics and delivering in a hospital.

Meet my Mama, she looked left and right to see if the road was clear, and dashed into a maize plantation nearby and pushed by herself: what a woman! She made it seem easier, this showed a woman born ready for her supernatural calling!

Women passing by heard a baby crying in the maize plantation and decided to check, they found my mother holding me tight and singing this song…

Fly, fly, fly my child
Fly, fly and touch the sky
Fly, fly , fly my child
Fly my Angel and light thy world.

The women sung and danced escorting mother and her daughter to the homestead.

'*Mwanamberi bayaye;Mwanamberi bayaye, Mwanamberi Nyeshikhoero..*"

It was joy all over. Mama was walking on the moon. My coming gave her joy and pride that no words could transcend.

One woman had rushed to the home to alert my grandmother and so she was expecting us. She started preparing 'amanyasi' for my birth and cleansing as it was supposed to.

July was a month of starvation and hunger! The famous luhya hunger season called, 'saba lulala' could be felt everywhere. There were no signs of smoke in the thatched round houses all over 'Mango' village. People preferred to eat at night only; this because food was scarce; no one wanted to cook during the day and they deliberately chose not to even to those who could afford, to avoid some visitors like "Indakwa" the pot bellied man who had big nose that could smell cooking food from miles; he would visit and stay until the scarce meal is served. Things were the same at my grandma's home, but since a visitor had arrived, she had to do something to welcome me in style. A feast was made and villagers invited to share the joy with mama....

Mama took time to also narrate her last night's dream to grandma. The desert in her dream symbolized the years of barrenness. The rain from the sky symbolized her broken water and of course the Angel was me, as explained by Sabina my good grandmother.

There and then, from mama's dream, I received my first name from my grandmother, Angelina; meaning Angel. My mother remembered the beam of light in her dream and automatically gave me my second name; 'Achieng' meaning sunshine. But I could not stop crying! The elderly women knew what that meant. "Time to take our granddaughter to her father for naming!" One of them instructed and so it was obeyed. My grandmother made presents for us which included wheat flour for my porridge, two hens for my mother to eat, maize flour, ripe banana and her own cotton blanket to cover me.

The women carried me as they sung and danced along the way until we arrived at our home. News travelled so fast and so my father had been told about my birth. His moods changed soon as he learned I was not a boy child. He instructed I be left at the gate first as Seruya, the village herbalist was invited and brought to speed of the events. She had to perform some rituals before I was allowed home. This was done with the intention to confuse the evil spirits that we may have encountered along the road; after that, Seruya picked me up and came with me to the homestead and gave me my third name; 'Awiti' which meant thrown away.........

"It all started with love; a love that was so kind and true. In her eyes was his future... Her lilting voice refreshing.... Her curves made eight his favourite number... Yes, a combination of Cleopatra and Venus were her beauty in his eyes... She was my good mother Sharon...!"

Chapter 2.

It all started like a hairy pimple on my back. In three weeks time, it had grown and started to worry my mother. She did not know what was happening to her only child.

"I think our daughter is unwell." Mama broached the subject to dad one evening for as it seemed, he never paid attention to me. My coming had made the two live like cats and ravens; dad came late and left very early. His attitude towards mama and I had changed from bad to worse. He was always busy; neglecting all his in the home.

So when Mama brought up this subject, she received a shock of her life. What dad replied did not only show that mama was alone in this, but she was also being accused of using dark magic to getting me. "She is your reward, now handle the curse on your own!" Dad shouted as he left the house that evening to return home the next day drunk and wasted.

The next thing mama received were kicks and blows for bringing the curse to his home. Dad had never raised his hands on my mother before, but he had learnt and perfected on this craft soon as I came to be.

The love he had for mama had faded, her lilting voice turned nagging, her curves were no longer appealing. She was alone. So like a hen that had hatched, mama took it upon herself come rain come sun to fight and protect me from the growing cold world towards her only child.

But he had let her down. A father is an epitome of strength and anchorage in the life of his child. He is the first provider of education to the life of his child: this education remains the key to the doors of a successful life this child awaits in the future.

It isn't easy in this modern culture to cultivate friendship because generally life has become too busy for such activities. But a father's attitude and language towards his children must at all times be friendly and soulful. He should be a true friend at all seasons and time. A correct peaceful ambiance is not necessarily needed for a child to get close to its father for any questions or advice, for in the voice of a father; the difference between bad and good is known by his children. In his voice; a child learns to respect the old and the young. Through a father's voice; a prediction of a bright future is brought close to reality to the life of his children. From a father's voice; a ch has a leader, provider and protector because a father's voice anchors authority and wires it in the system of his children.

The next day, mama decided to take me to hospital for medical check-up. But back at home, dad had called his village elders to discuss on how they would do away with what was viewed as a curse that could devour his entire family. What shocked the minority elites in town who heard of this was the fact that in this day and time, with dad's education, he still believed in those retrogressive and backward laws of the past.

"Hello Mrs. Kwale, my name is Dr Aseka." The doctor handling my case introduced himself. I had started to grow pale and weak. More than anything else, Mama just wanted me to live.

"It is a pleasure 'daktari', what is wrong with my baby?" Mama went straight to the reason why she was there. As it seemed, she was not there for pleasantries. She really wanted to find a solution to what could save both her child and marriage. Despite dad's change of attitude and even his new violent nature, Mama still had faith in her marriage. She chose to see a half full glass as opposed to the reduced water. She chose to keep fighting for her marriage. Mama knew how important a complete family would be to me. She knew the importance of a father and mother in the life of a child.

Maybe what kept her into this was even the fact that she had seen how broken homes destroys innocent children's lives. Most parents at a point of breakups fail to consider the children who end up suffering and left with permanent scars that don't heal. Her wish therefore was to fight from within for the sake of my future wellbeing.

In the doctor's office, tension had started to grow. The look on his face and even how he started to speak, one could easily tell that he had bad news. He opened what seemed like an envelope that had my medical report, readjusted his reading glasses and started to read as he explained the findings to mama. "We have done several tests to the baby, and we are sorry to report that baby Angel was born with a severe birth defect called, 'spina bifida'. This is a type of neural tube defect; a condition that affects the spine and is usually apparent at birth.."

He continued, "This happens anywhere along the spine if the neural tube does not close all the way, thus the backbone that protects the spinal cord does not form and close as it should. This often results in damage to the spinal cord and nerves. The condition might cause physical and intellectual disabilities that range from mild to severe."

At this point, my mother's hands were on her head and you could see streams of tears from her eyes. I doubt she was even listening. It was so painful to hear such words coming from the doctor. The doctor requested her to calm down as he continued to explain. "The severity depends on the type of 'spina bifida'. According to the tests done, Angelina was suffering from the most severe of all; 'Myelomeningocele', as a matter of fact, when people talk about 'spina bifida', most often they are referring to 'myelomeningocele'; With this condition, a sac of fluid comes through an opening in the baby's back. Part of the spinal cord and nerves are in this sac and are damaged as you can see from the baby's back. This type of 'spina bifida' causes moderate to severe disabilities, such as problems affecting how the person goes to the bathroom, loss of feeling in the person's legs or feet, and not being able to move the legs. I am sorry."

This was hard for mama to stomach. She was already weeping like I had already died. The doctor asked her to take some minutes before she could come for more recommendations. But mama had had enough that she did not want a break. She whipped her tears. "Doctor, help my child. I will do all it takes to see my daughter well!" She held the doctor's hands and begged him to help me. As it seemed, he held the key to the peaceful marriage she envisioned before accepting to my father. This doctor held the key to my bright future.

"I am so sorry to report that, this condition had no cure. At the speed in which it is growing, baby Angelina might not make it to next month. It will financially and emotionally drain you for no reason. As a doctor, I will recommend euthanasia."

Even before he could finish, mama was screaming on top of her lungs while her hands were already on the doctor's throat. She grabbed it so tight and squeezed with all the energy She had. The doctor was in shock, he was almost chocking to his last breathe when a nurse heard the altercation plus mama's voice and came to the rescue of the poor doctor! "You will not kill my baby! Shameless man!" Mama shouted as she picked me up and left the hospital charged and rattled like a snake. She was ready to attack. She was ready to take life of it means preserving mine.

As she walked from the hospital to our home, her hopes of rekindling the lost spark in her marriage had faded. She stared at me without a clue of how she would help me. It was us against the bitter World. Mama had no idea how she would tell this to my father. Little did she know that a court of public opinion had been set at our home ready to read its verdict without trial. It was a mob justice.

Dad had already invited village elders including grandma. They were expecting us. As mama was moving her almost dead body to the meeting, the 'bench' was waiting for her like scavengers waiting for the cocas to fall before they descend on it. Mama sat on the empty chair at the front that was waiting for her. In this court, one had no right to an attorney, the accused had no right to fair trail or hearing.

"My brothers and sisters, elders of our land, greetings to you all." Atako, the village spokesman stood to start the meeting. He was a middle aged man who knew how to manipulate and play with words to the amusement of them who were his audience. This role therefore was not given to him in vain. Here, his role was simple, to read the accusations before a final verdict is given out by the council of elders.

But in what seemed like a change of tactics, he changed the script and said, "a cock will not crow at night, and if it does, there is a reason, we are here because it has happened. Because our wife is here and she is from the hospital, let her tell us her findings before we can decide on the fate of the child. Welcome our wife." He spoke handing over the stage to Mama. This had never been witnessed in such meetings. But mama was not a fool to fall for his trap. She knew it was a trap.

"My husbands, my mothers, elders of our community, greetings to you all." Mama took the stage. She had cried enough, and at this point, she had to stand strong and represent her case having been fortunate enough to get that precious opportunity. She was a very confident and eloquent woman, this complemented her bold eyes and strong personality. She was respected all over the town and was always invited to share her thoughts on issues affecting the community. This time it was in her house and she had a chance to present her case in a way that would make and not break her family; for as a woman, she was there to build and not to destroy her home.

She continued, "an unborn child that laughs in its mother's belly when the mother is being chased by a hyena, is an unwise child; this matter touches and puts to test our moral fabric as a community. It therefore isn't me or my daughter against you but it affects all of u." At this point, most of her audience felt lost. They expected a heated   battle, but she took a different angle. Her aim was to appeal to their conscious mind.

She continued, "I have been childless for the three decades that I have been your wife here. I have endured the pain of not being able to bless my husband with the fruit of my womb! I became a laughing stock in the whole village, even as my very own husband went further to prove to the whole world that he was not the problem and this hurt me so bad. I took the bitter pill, for is it not the function of a woman to submit to the will of her husband? Is it not her calling to accept anything that makes her husband happy? I remained loyal and submissive to my husband. I served him well like I was well trained by my mother. But my elders and husbands, is it not God who gives children? Where are children manufactured so that we can all go and buy these precious gifts to our satisfaction?" The whole crowd broke into laughter. Tension seemed to have subsided. She knew she had a number of them on the palm of her hands.

"Now that my husband is here, let him confirm to you that my daughter is not his child and I give you my word, I will leave this place knowing what my mistakes are; should I be blamed for giving birth to an innocent sick child? Should this young innocent child be subject of such gathering without care or protection? Our daughter needs us now more than ever! I need your help! Please forgive me if I may have said anything that I should have not, but I need your help." Mama spoke with passion. She sat down holding me tight in her arms.

"When a man's house is on fire, he will not have time to chase on rats!" My father cleared his throat as it was his turn to address the gathering. " Elders and my fellow brothers, the matter at hand is a closed issue; I have twenty tow daughters and one son; have you seen any of them resembling this young girl? Have you my brothers ever witnessed such a case in our bloodline? The gods of our land have spoken loud and he that fights the gods is a dead meat. I choose life! I refuse to be called the father: I leave the matter to the able council of our elders who are the voices of the gods!" The whole meeting went mum. You could hear a pin drop! My mother was in shock. When mama was speaking, it felt like she had managed to grab few of her listeners to her side, but when dad took the stage, he managed to neutralize the emotions that mama had evoked. But more was yet to come..

My grandmother stood to give her thoughts on the matter. Mama thought that she would take her side but she did not, she suggested I be thrown away to the forest, and my mother to be cleansed from the curse that could eat all her children. Such a case had never been witnessed and these people were conservatives who knew nothing about science and paid no attention to it. The verdict was out. I had been found guilty of two counts: first and gracious of all, I was born a girl, and second, I was sick. This amounted to excommunication and so I had to face it..

After carefully listening to both sides, the Chief elder stood and recommended I be thrown away; this was seconded by almost everyone including my grandmother. As it seemed, it was the world against me and my mother. This was a cut in my mother's liver. She did not expect to hear such utterances coming especially from her own mother. That was betrayal of the highest level.

Before all these, my parents had had a good relationship. Mama loved my father so much that she put up with all the humiliation she started facing the moment dad realized that she was not giving her babies. He was incited to marry a second wife but he chose twenty three, both of whom were never introduced to anyone but the children he had with them. This hurt my mother but again she chose to stay and fight from within.

Every person is infinitely more vast in scope than what appears to the naked eyes. For that reason, to have a great sense of who we are and where we are heading to, we have to employ a point of view that is penetrating and catches like radar, to notice the images that might pass unnoticed; one such image is of a parent in the lives of their children. They are an invisible world that strongly affects the visible worlds of their children. Parents bring the past flavours of life, hidden family traditions on to the table of the children's lives. A child who lacks these figures is permanently divided and alienated from its physical world. Mama never wanted to see this happening to me.

She had lived long enough and witnessed these things happen to innocent children all over. As a woman of faith, she owed it to her God to fulfil her motherly duties to me which included sacrificing her own happiness for my sake.

According to Mama, every single child that is born is a gift from God. That child must be allowed to grow and fulfil its purpose on earth and has a right to an inclusive parenting from both its biological parents and the society at large. For it takes a village to raise a child. For that reason, any decision to have or not have a child should be made before conception because after; then it is to be given a chance to see the world, live in a home full of love so that the child can become that which God created it to be. No child is a mistake!

But this evening was different. Mama said no! She carried me in her arms, and like a lioness charged ready to attack anyone who would put their hands on me; she pushed herself out of the crowd and ran as fast as her legs could carry her. And like the biblical mother to Moses, mama had to make a tough decision to hide me from the world; this with one aim; to protect me......
how I wish she did it differently though…

*But love fades, so it faded: love ends, so it ended: the sweet voice turned nagging... Her
curves not appealing... A tree planted: THE SEED UNWANTED! Angelina the Angel,
Achieng the sun, Awiti the rejected seed I became! In his home girls were unwanted; stone
for his sling he wanted! Rejected at birth: left for the hard earth!*

Chapter 3.

'The Fountain of Peace' Children's home stood at the heart of 'Mambo Leo' estate in the big city. It was one of the biggest children's facility hosting more than two hundred street children and orphans. It also purported to support the less privileged bright students in the community through scholarships and bursaries. This became my second home.

After patient mismanagement and loving neglect, my parent's marriage came to an end that fateful evening when I was rejected by everyone who was supposed to care and protect me.

Mama could not take it anymore. She had reached an extension limit: every human has one. What added more pain to the injury was the fact that her own mother did not take her side.

Mother-child relationship is not essentially a Union of personalities like other friendships but rather an attraction and magnetism of the soul. The relationship begins from conception and through the working of fate, after nine months, it blossoms and its bloom extends on earth. Most mothers will put themselves in front to protect and fight for their children. It is rare to see otherwise; and so when mama saw that everyone was against her including her very own mother, she decided to move out to Kakamega Town to seek help from her best friend Sali.

My mother came from a family that never cared about the education of a girl child. The girl child was only used as a tool for finding wealth through dowry; and in return, she was supposed to give birth to massage the egos of the man she got married to. Those days, the place of a woman was in the kitchen, on bed and on the pieces of land. Figuring this out and the fact that her lack of education landed her to subordination and a prisoner in the name of marriage, my mother said no! She walked out for good.

She stepped on the ground four times with her bare feet, keeping her mind focused to the love she had for me and the need to see me blossom, she took her pride and beauty and lowered them under her feet, all this with one aim; to unclip my wings.

Mama found herself as a maid in her best friend's house. She had no option but to swallow this bitter truth for my sake.

Things started to change between the two friends. Of course one was now the servant of the other. Sali' attitude towards my mother and I changed.

She could use funny names to refer to us. Mama was given a name, 'yawar' a luo slung to mean someone in need of help always. No one spared my innocence as a one month old child. I received Insults from the society. No one wanted to carry the 'curse' apart from mama. I was always on her back as she did her maid duties.

All the pain in my mother's heart were washed off by rain drops in the evening on her way back to the one room iron sheet house that she had rented in town.

With all these struggles and suffering, it took the efforts, love and the determination of a woman to see me live to see the next sun. My mother brushed off the insults and vowed to only focus on the goal at hand.

But things did not go well as planned. One day, Sali attempted to slap my mother over unwashed dishes. I had fallen ill and I needed urgent medical care. Mama was forced to rush me to hospital. Sali did not understand this. It was at this point in time when Mama could not take it any longer, she did not fight back, but left the house plus the friendship that had collected dust.

I never had the pleasure of knowing my mother; other than the picture she left behind plus a journal that had the story of my birth, my roots and a letter which I will share later.

In the facility, we only knew one woman; Mrs. Asewe as our mother. Most of the time, in our tiny thoughts and mind, we could not help but ask questions how this woman managed to mother all of us. We referred to her as mother; until one day when she was disciplining one of us and when he cried calling her mother, she shouted: "I am not your mother!" the whole room became silent and confused.

I became curious. I wanted more answers in regards to how we came to be. One evening, I went to the matron's office and requested to talk to her. "Why did you say you not our mother?" I went straight to the questions even without greetings. I was only eight years old so I didn't know much about etiquette.

"I don't know if you are ready for this information child, but come tomorrow after your morning devotion, I would like to show you something." Apparently, her tone suggested that she had not taken my request wrongly.

That night was the longest night of my entire life. I don't remember sleeping at all.

Our hall of residence was divided into small cubicles each holding a maximum of four beds. It was tiny. That made it too hot more so at night. In such a situation, one would feel comfortable if they slept without covering up; but the mosquitoes did not allow such arrangements. One had to choose wisely. So that night, you can imagine I went through all the torture without a blink of my eyes.

I was the first person to wake up the following day. This was unlike me. Everyone knew that I loved my sleep. But on that day, it was different. I wanted to know the truth so much but I dreaded it. Sometimes fear is a saviour that most of us never recognize; it makes one live longer. Truth they say hurts and kills faster, but I'll say, those things that we don't know are the ones that get us killed. They are like a cancer that spreads slowly taking us down bit by bit; much as I feared it, I wanted the whole truth.

Immediately after my morning devotion, I was on the matron's door. She was expecting me. "I will not take much of your time child." She cleared her throat before handing me an old looking brown envelope. It was a bit heavy for what I thought could be in.

"Here is what you are looking for. I will leave you in here to go through the information then join you later." She gave me a long look before closing the door behind her. The truth was finally there. I wish she could have stayed to help me out. I was alone….. But what was in the envelop? Why couldn't she share verbally..?

The first eight years of my life were like hell on earth. I remember how nature forced me to grow faster because the facility was crowded and resources were sparse; it was survival for the fittest, fastest and strongest just like in the jungle. Kids who were physically disabled had even more challenges; no one spared their innocence or cared about their disabilities; they were expected to fight for survival just like other kids; I was among the disabled kids in the home.

The birth defect had affected my speech and legs. I was not crippled but I had to use crutches to move around because my legs were weak thus affecting my balance. I also had dyslexia; a condition that made it difficult for me to read, or write properly; I was a slow learner. I grew up feeling like everything was working against me. I had no friends and kept to myself. One would confuse me to an introvert; but I was not; no one wished to associate with me; I used to admire other kids who were able to run and play games around.

Every evening after school, each one of us was assigned a special specific duty meant to generate income for the food, clothes and medicine that we got from the facility. Education was free: the only free but most expensive thing that I knew at the moment. So those of us who were a little older were given heavier duties like selling charcoal or clothes around the streets.

Those who were younger like me and disabled were given ground-nuts to sell but under someone's supervision.

The more you sold determined the favour you'll receive from the matron. Sometimes I slept on an empty stomach when I couldn't meet her expectations. Sometimes she will beat us up or scold us before giving us something to eat.

What never added up was the fact that after all she did to us, she was the one who shared the word of God to us every morning before we started our day. "People can really change so fast", we used to whispered to ourselves. Apparently, She was everything in there and we had no option but to accept the horrible truth.

Another thing that never added up was the fact that we received donations of; food; clothes and beddings from various none governmental organizations; but we never saw them. When these visitors came in, we were made to look pitiful and unkempt to capture attention and make them donate more. Sometimes we were told to put on rugs and pose for photographs that were sent abroad to seek help that we never saw. We had to work for food every evening.

So I slowly opened the envelope. In there was a small good News Bible. In the middle, I remember very well, the paper had been folded and placed in my favorited books in the Bible: The Ephesians. I had many reasons to believe that my mother wanted me to always read the book: She wanted me to become a good lady, a responsible one. That was the first bible verse that I ever read in my life.

But before I understood the mystery behind the Bible verses, I had a letter to read. Here it is:

" To my Angel,

If you are reading this letter, it only means that my dreams for you came true. My daughter, when I first held you, I fell for your beautiful soul; you were so adorable and full of life: my first fruit of the womb. But child, Sometimes when you love someone, you have to let go for the person to be safe.

I loved your father, But things didn't work out between us. I don't want you to take the easy way out like I did, but if you ever do, I want you to know that, there is no reason for dying if you never lived my girl. God gave you amazing strength and a beautiful soul, through you I know that His great works shall be fulfilled: that's why you must not take the easy way out: you must live my child.

As you live, and as life offers you its turns and twists, never allow it to pin or clip you: Soar my Angel. Don't live your life crying or trying to understand why I left, don't waste your life hating your father for his choice either, live your life my daughter, for bitterness and hate are like snakes in your soul; they devour you day to day. Enjoy everything that life offers you. Respect everyone even the weak ones. Love your God and live by his teachings and wisdom. I believe you are safe where I left you. Read that book and understand it. In there lays the wisdom that you seek. Till we meet again, I cherish you my love.

Your mother; Sharon."

My mother left me at the gate of this premises. It is said that she threw herself on an oncoming vehicle and died on the spot.

I was left for the world. How sure was she that I will survive? Can such extreme measures be used to justify her love for me? I was rejected at birth; my wings clipped, and this broke me eternally….. It became a scar that could not heal; a vacuum that no human could fill; the sky that do not touch the ground; a square that is not round; the dead that do not produce a sound; and the lost in my life that were never to be found…

I remember that day like it was today; the 16th day of March 2010. I woke up feeling tired and restless. I had sobbed about my situation for a year now. The truth of the matter is that this had drained me both mentally, emotionally and physically. I had become weaker and never took my classes serious. I had no reason to live. I felt like I was alone and more than anything, I wanted to take my mother's path. So I wrote the following note.

" A New path has been formed,
Unexpectedly it came but welcomed,
What I feel for this one cannot be explained.
Words don't transcend this level of tie,
Too complex are my feelings like the stars in the sky,
How can I stop a butterfly from flapping its wings?
Am I chasing a kite that has cut its strings?
Love is often spoken but seldom found,
It isn't perfect neither is it blind,
For it sees with more clarity than our human eyes,
I see why you left and why I must sublime like dry ice,
Our human imperfections had clouded my vision but now I see,
I will not live your dreams neither will I continue sleeping,
I choose this path and on your footsteps I'm walking,
Till we meet again;

Angelina."

I left the note on my bed and went to look for a perfect tool that will facilitate my journey back 'home'. No sooner had I left the room than the matron came in. I may have no explanation to her unexpected visit to our room that morning. She saw the note and took it. When I came back to the room with a rope, I found her reading the note and I couldn't be blind to the streams of tears all over her face. She wasn't crying because of the message therein because she did not understand the metaphor; but the fact that she never thought I could write that fluently and deep.

But when she saw me standing at the door with a rope in my hands, that is when she started to comprehend the message on the text. Mrs. Asewe ran towards me and gave me a big hug. I was shocked. I could not move.

"No my child, no!" Those were the only words she spoke. She cried hugging me for awhile, then supported me to her office. And so I lived to see the sun again………….

Chapter 4.

I had stayed in there for almost a decade: nine years and six months to be specific. I was now grown and could see things with more clarity. Even the same, part of me was still yearning to know my roots. I wanted to know my father; I wanted to know my grandma: I wanted to listen to their side of story; In other words, my heart was yearning for the solid truth.

One day, on the 16th of May 2011, I decided that enough was enough. In there I was like a caged bird. How else would I know where I'm heading to unless I knew where I'm coming from? I waited until it was the right time. We had been sent to the streets for our daily tasks. I took a chance and that was my last day in the facility. The truth of the matter is, in the children's home, our presence there was only valuable when donors came or when posing for pictures to attract donations from abroad. The other times we were viewed as liabilities. So when you leave, no one looked for you. No one cared if you were dead or alive. I found myself on the streets. At first I started to regret:

"Whose dog will I call my friend? Whose door will I knock for shelter and love? Whose dustbin will I call my plate?"

The streets were more cruel for the new bird. Other street kids saw me as their rival who had come to compete for the limited space. I was twelve at that time.

I had developed a love for poetry and singing. I loved writing poems. In my new hobby I found closure and company in the cold at night. I recited them loud on the streets and that's how I got food to eat.

But I had a plan: My aim was to raise funds that would facilitate me in going to find my roots. I thought it would be easy, but as it were, with my disability and new territory, I experienced the hardness of the earth literally.

What seemed like a ray of hope stroke me when least expected. I was in front of a mall doing my usual singing for handouts. These couple just came from nowhere and felt moved by my poem; read it bellow..

'Times are hard, I want you as a friend to call,
Armies have formed against me but you are behind me tall,
Even if they strike me down, I know you will catch me when I fall,
For you did it yesterday; you will do it again my unchangeable God!'

"That was a beautiful piece young girl, what's your name?" The lady asked extending her hands to shake mine which were filthy. "My name is Angelina Achieng Awiti!" I replied with lots of confidence. She introduced herself as Mrs. Hannah Kusimba and the gentleman beside her who was her husband as Mr. Anthony Kusimba.

They took me to the mall and offered to buy me a burger. I was so hungry that I gobbled the meal like a pig. I did not care who was watching. After which, the couple listened to my story and offered to help. They requested to take me to their home. At that point in time, I had no option but to accept the offer. It was a ladder I needed to accomplish my goal. I couldn't hide the joy. I was finally off the streets. So I said these words to myself:

'I was on a crossroad, but like a flash of light, my God opened my ways and gave me hope!'

Mr. Anthony opened the back door of his black Mercedes G-Class for me. I just could not help but feel class and opulence at its best. The soft leather seats made me feel like I was in the middle of the ocean in a yatch. As we continued moving, I thought my eyes had seen enough until my attention got drawn to the quiet and serene lash environment that led us to this huge palatial home. The green well manicured lawns plus the big beautiful bungalow came to agreement with the fact that these people were wealthy.

I had no idea where we were but it felt good for a change. I was introduced to Ashley who was the help. She was ordered to show me the guest room. The room was painted pink, and had all manner of beautiful decorations. The bed was a queen size with soft mattress and pillows. At first, I felt like I was dreaming. My attention was brought back to reality when Ashley asked me to go to the bathroom and take a shower. God knows I needed it; I looked like a cow that had just gotten out of a dip. After the warm shower, Ashley gave me some warm clothes and asked me to come downstairs for dinner. It was 7pm.

That night was the best night that I ever had since I was born. For the first time in my life I had other wars to fight and not fights with mosquitoes at night; this environment was not conducive for their breeding; the cosiness alone acted as a bug repellent. "Money is good! I want to have it all! I want to never go back to the streets again!" I said to myself.

I didn't know what time I slept, but I was woken up by a beautiful aroma of bacon coming from the kitchen. Ashley was up and she was doing her magic. I freshened up and found my way to the kitchen. She was so good to me and we automatically became friends. I had lived a lonely life. I never had the pleasure of having someone to talk to or just trust in the warmth of a true friend..

A new chapter had been presented to me and as it seemed, it was a chapter of hope. This hope was sealed when Mr. and Mrs. Kusimba agreed to fully adopt me and take me in as their very own child. The two had no children of their own.

I was taken back to school. I left the children's home in class eight. Because of the delays, I had to repeat class seven. This was not a bad idea.

My first two years with the Kusimbas were amazing. I remember I had forgotten about my past. I sat for my class eight national finals and I did very well scoring marks that gave me an opportunity to join Pangani girls high school…

My past ghost started to haunt me the moment I joined high school. I had gained strength in my feet but I still had difficulties in communicating fluently. Things changed one fateful day when I had gone back home for midterm break. Mrs. Kusimba had taken a business trip to Sydney. When I arrived home, I realised that the place was so cold. Ashley looked so different and afraid. As a young girl, it took me long before I could comprehend what was going on.

To date, I still haven't cleared the horrific shame that I felt that night. I was sleeping in my room when I had some brawl in the kitchen. Curiously I moved slowly to go see what was happening. It could have been better if Mr. Kusimba didn't see me, but our eyes met. The shock in his eyes plus confusion made him numb. He could not move. Ashley was crying in pain as he held her mouth tight.

I closed the kitchen door as first as I could and struggled to get to my room. The next thing I felt was a strong grip on my arm. "If I ever hear anything of what you just saw anywhere, you are a dead meat!" Mr. Kusimba was breathing fire. He was like a rattled snake. I had never ever thought I'll ever be that scared in my life. The warning sent a chill in my spine. I could not move. He left me and went to his room.

It became the second longest night of my life. I just couldn't bring myself to the fact that I witnessed someone I had loved and looked up to as my muse taking advantage of my friend and his help. I felt guilty about it. I didn't know how to help Ashley. As a matter of course, I knew I'll never be able to look at my Foster father in the eye again. This act made me start to imagine what my mother could have been going through. At some point I found myself justifying the decision my mother had taken. I sobbed all night. I woke up with a migraine. My eyes were swollen and I just could not get out of my room. Maybe I was too ashamed or I was afraid to face both my father and Ashley.

But the silence in the house really scared me more. Nothing seemed to be going on in the house. The usual morning aroma from the kitchen was absent. That's when it occurred to me that maybe the worse had happened.

I gathered the little strength I had and walked to the kitchen. It was in a mess. The unwashed utensils plus some blood stains on the floor made me even more sick.

Something that looked like a paper caught my attention on the far side of the kitchen counter. Indeed it was a note addressed to two people. The folded top side was addressed to me in bold and it read, "ANGELINA, PLEASE MAKE SURE THIS NOTE IS GIVEN TO MRS. KUSIMBA. GOODBYE!"

The last thing I remember was something hitting my head so hard. I woke up later to find myself on the floor. I had passed out. This news was so shocking that my feet could not carry me. I fell on the floor but I did not injure myself.

For the second time in my life, I found myself on a crossroad. I didn't know what to do or how to handle the situation I just found myself in. I did not want to be the person to separate my Foster parents, but again, in my heart of hearts, I wanted justice for Ashley. My education and my life was on the line. I had to choose wisely. For the three day midterm break that I was home, after the incident, we never saw eye to eye with Mr. Kusimba. I kept the note very safe in my school bag. I carried it with me to school. Sincerely, I did not read it.

In school, my teachers noticed a sudden change in behaviour. I kept it to myself most of the time. This made my class teacher Mrs. Atonya to call me one morning. She was so good at what she did that nothing could escape her attention. She was the first person to realise I was not ok. The approach she used made me open up to her. My story really moved her and she promised to look into it and give me a solid solution the next day.

I remember the next day I was taking breakfast when I saw Mrs. Kusimba's car packed in the school parking area. She came very early. This sent a cold chill in my body. I later learnt that it is Mrs. Atonya who had invited her to come. We met in the deputy's office.

I was asked to speak the truth so that we could help Ashley and also protect me from the dangers that lay ahead. Never in my wildest dreams have I ever thought I would be in such a situation. I was between a rock and a hard place. But again, I did not want to commit the sin of omission. I knew I had powers in my hands to change the situation and help my friend Ashley.

I had no strength to speak but I gave out the letter to Mrs. Kusimba. We came to learn that Ashley had gone through similar series of acts for so long. She was put in a family way at some point and forced to terminate the seed.

Mr. Kusimba was a defaulter tree. Usually, these trees will bare fruits but never care where the fruits end up.

Every seed is special irrespective of how it came to be. The seeds are alive because of the will of God and only Him who gives life has a right to take. The seeds have a right to be placed in the right soils, planted and cared for until they bloom and fulfil their divine purpose on earth. No human hand should ever take this right away.

So, this revelation set me free, but it came with a big price I knew I must pay. That cup was too big for me but like the biblical son of man; I had to drink through it.

First, the long arm of the law finally caught up with Mr. Kusimba. This was good news to me. He was arraigned and charged for defilement and also conducting unauthorized termination of the seed. He was sentenced to ten years in prison without bail.

Second, my Foster parent's marriage came to an end. I was caught up in the middle and at that point in time, none of them paid attention to me. I had no idea how bad things had escalated until the time when schools closed. I went home to find the biggest shock of my life, the house had been auctioned and had new tenants. Mrs. Kusimba had travelled abroad and I had nowhere to go.

I thought I had found myself a family. These people were so good to me. I just couldn't come to terms with the fact that none of them had me in mind while making their decisions. Indeed the heavy burdens of the mighty will always rest upon the shoulders of the weak. It also goes without saying, those who have no share in the fortunes of the affluent have a share in their misfortunes.

I found myself back to the streets in school uniforms. I had been bitten twice; a heavy cloud of confusion blurred my eyes; though I had no option but to again teach my heart to sublime like dry ice; and like a gambler on the streets cast my dice; hoping to finally have my desires fulfilled; the wishes to see my real parents; to finally put away the doubts and hate that was breeding in my heart towards men; and to finally understand the real meaning of family. These things I yearned for....

Chapter 5.

Where we stay sometimes is not where we belong: Our permanent place of residence is where we hope for: is where our minds reside: is where our thoughts call home; at that point in my life, I chose to imagine a perfect home for myself and all the street children.

As I walked in the heavy downpour, I switched off my conscious mind and embraced stoicism ; I became deaf and dump to the pain I was going through; for the first time in my life I stopped thinking about myself: I thought about the children in the Children's Home; I thought about the pain they all endure to survive; I thought about their unseen tears in the rain.

My home was in my mind. Each step that I made that evening had a prayer request: I invoked the heavens to open and by its gracious mercy, take my street family from the choking years of abject poverty, the murky spheres of hopelessness and the shackles of misfortunes that weighed heavily on our backs.

I felt like God had patiently neglected us to live and die in indigence: I felt like we were children of a lesser god: "in whose door shall we knock for love and shelter? In whose arms shall we run for protection? In whose dustbin shall we find a plate?" I kept lamenting and praying this time in a loud voice!

I didn't care who was listening or who paid attention. Moreover, it was raining heavily so no one was listening.

I remembered Mary, a middle aged woman who found herself and her four sons on the streets. This Amazing woman was beautiful, but her natural beauty was covered in a cloud of hopelessness and lack; one could notice wrinkles on her face, a sure indication that poverty and time were indeed the greatest enemy to beauty.

Even the same, she could still walk on the runway of wisdom, strong faith, strength in character, devotion to her children, fidelity to her stand as a woman: and still win the contest! Mary never gave us reasons to doubt her strength as a woman. She never accepted handouts either, but ate from her sweat. She could leave her four sons behind and go beg for opportunities to wash offices: just for food. This hustle gave her joy at the end of the day as she saw her children full; this was her sacred duty and supernatural calling.

It is in such stories and bravery that I found hope. I knew that I will see the light. I had hope for a better tomorrow.

My feet were moving, but I had no clear knowledge of where I was or heading to. I was tired; tired of being nature's punching bag; I was tired of poverty; I was tired of the streets; I was tired of humanity. I didn't know who else I could trust. Every smile I received from the world was conceived and conceptualised in my mind as the biblical serpent's head that had an apple but sharp fangs behind ready to sink in Eve's skin. I had been broken and it would take a real potter's touch to craft me back to my whole self.

I could not stop moving nor crying. I was in the middle of the road. I did not know where he came from, but he held me so tight, he just didn't let go. I found myself in his car. "Young girl, where are you coming from at this hour? Do you want to die? What is your name?" The man asked. I couldn't take my eyes off him.

He was a very handsome young man in his early twenties. He was tall, dark and very attractive. He smelt so good and he spoke with a rich manly voice. I honestly forgot what his question was. I just kept looking in his eyes. Maybe because I was looking for answers. Maybe because this was the last human who would either make or break me completely. Maybe because I was in love with a stranger. At my age and that stage in life, all human morals were against me having those crazy thoughts. But there I was, with this good looking young man who almost hit me with his car. I just kept staring at him; our eyes glued to one another..

He held my hands and said, "never mind, just tell me where I can drop you!" These words reminded me of my misfortunes. And I started to cry again. I didn't know how he did it, but to be honest, I just didn't care if he would hurt me or not. On the contrary, he was a true gentle soul. A true angel in my darkest hour. He was heaven sent. He wiped my tears and asked me to permit him to buy me a cup of coffee. As we drove in the rain to the nearby java house, I couldn't help but keep on admiring this stranger. We never spoke award in the twenty minutes drive.

That is how I met Alpha; a fourth year medical student at the University of Nairobi.

He had rented his own studio apartment in Parkland-Nairobi. The fact that he was a student, driving and had a clean well furnished apartment made it clear that he was from a well to do family.

I just loved how he paid attention to every word I spoke without saying a word. He listened carefully and the only thing he could do was to sip his coffee in a well mannered way and nod his head. We arrived at the Java house at exactly 8pm and we were the last customers to leave; as a matter of fact, we were asked to politely leave because it was 12am. All these hours, Alpha never said a word nor took his eyes off mine. I spoke my heart and he was a good listener.

Because it was late, he decided to take me to his place. And to my surprise, this man gave me his bed while he slept on the couch. At first, I was afraid but he assured me through actions that I was safe. I think that is what I needed at that point in life; someone who will not just speak but through action show me that there were still good humans out there.

I found myself staying with my new friend for three weeks before schools opened.

Alpha never took advantage of me in any way. At some point I wondered if truly he was straight or in the closet. This show of respect and maturity in how he treated me sparked a friendship that was never to be broken.

We could talk about everything. We laughed most of the time. Apart from being mature and striking good looking, he was also a good cook. I never knew how to cook; but in his kitchen I learned this important woman's tool of trade; slowly he taught me how to love and appreciate myself for who I was.

He offered to see me through my education and this gave me wings to fly. He became my true guardian angel; my ladder holder; my muse; my best friend.

What I didn't know, is that I had fallen deeply in love with him. I never showed it, but it was love at first glance. There was a strong mutual attraction between us. I could see in the way we talked and how easy we were with each other.

Few years passed until I just felt it was time to let the poor gentle soul sleep in the bed with me. I must admit that in the four years that we shared the bed, of course when I came for holiday breaks, Alpha never put his hands on me inappropriately. He respected our space and this made me more attracted to him; it also made me change the bad perception I had about men while growing up.

He later graduated with a first class honours degree in Medicine while I joined the University of Nairobi to study journalism; something I came to learn later that it was rooted in my DNA; this was my father's career; indeed an apple never falls far from the tree.

It was at this point in our lives when we started having deep conversations about ourselves. I had grown fond of him and the feelings were mutual. For the years that we stayed together, I had never seen him introduce me to any woman or disrespect our space by bringing one.

It is the simplest things that I saw in him that made me fall so deep in love with him. I just wanted him for keeping. But before anything else, I requested him to help me locate my roots. That way, I would be a free soul.

On the 6th day of February 2017, we started the journey back home. I still had the written journal with me that had the exact location of where I came from. I had never shared it with Alpha until this date.

What seemed like a journey to my self discovery ended up with a shock of my life. Alpha realised some similarities in the names of our father plus the village the note said I had come from. I noticed in his sudden change of attitude but he tried his best not to show me or tell me anything. He too was in shock.

We arrived at Ndula Village in the evening. The note directed us to exactly where Alpha came from and where his parents were buried.

Your guess is right, It turned out to be that Alpha was actually my step brother. This explains the strong bond that we felt for each other. This explains the respect that naturally was between us.

"Then came Alpha, a fine looking gent; beautiful smile with an attractive scent; my saviour my pride: my protector my fortress to hide: he saved me from the cold: and this is how it had to unfold...

It was love at first glance, a force that swept me off my balance; it was swift and fit: and so I fell deep and wanted him for keep!

But no! Not again! The rejected seed fell near its parent's tree! Abomination!"

It was so sad that I never had a chance to meet both my grandma and my father, but I felt warm to be home; my real home: It felt sad that I never got a chance to marry the love of my life; but it was so uplifting to have him as a brother and a best friend. I got a chance to know more about my mother and reunited with my other siblings.

Golden Pen had collected dust and was on the ground but we owed to our departed loved ones to bring it back to life. I slowly found closure and chose to forgive my parents. This to me was a gift that I could not trade with anything in this world: for I held it deep in my heart for the rest of my living….

- **THE END**.

AUTHOR'S NOTES AND THOUGHTS.

A relationship that has gone sour but a child is involved has a fare share of bad endings. The endings sometimes inflicts negative and permanent wounds to the life of this child if the people involved are not mature. The endings can also be a permanent ghost in the after life of the parties involved. The past relationships at times haunts and hurts the future relationships.

Angelina and Alpha finds themselves in this.

With an aim to reach the sky, humanity makes us blind to the flowers that blossom beneath our feet. We neglect our families in the name of making our careers grow to earn big positions at our places of work. We assume our wives at home because on our minds we are carried away by some other women, who we blindly think are better than our own. We neglect our parents simply because we feel we are big enough to take care of ourselves. The list of our ignorance is endless.

Facts be told, no man has ever beaten gravity. So as we try to fly higher away from our homes in the name of finding greater things in life, gravity sends us back to the earth where we belong. Funny thing is that the same flowers that we stepped on trying to find a ground for flight are always there to welcome us back.

The greatest form of punishment an individual can ever get isn't death but regrets from the ignorance of the people he knows will always be there for him.

Guard these flowers, water them, love them and they will for ever beautify your world.

The word father according to my understanding means: provider, giver, protector, founder and the head of a family.

Every person is infinitely more vast in scope than what appears to the naked eyes. For that reason, to have a great sense of who we are and where we are heading to, we have to employ a microscopic eye, a point of view that is penetrating and catches like radar, to notice the images that might pass unnoticed; one such image is a father in a family.

The image of a father plus his influence in the growth of a child is something never to be avoided. In poetry I compare it to an invisible world that strongly affects our visible worlds. A father brings past flavour of life, our hidden family traditions, our whole being on the table of our lives. A child who lacks this figure is permanently divided and alienated from his physical world. See how Angelina struggles because of the absence of this important figure in her life.

Every single child that is born is a gift from God. That child must be allowed to grow and fulfil his purpose on earth and he has a right to an inclusive parenting both from his biological parents and the society at large. Yes, It takes a village to raise a child. For that reason, any decision to have or not have a child should be made before conception because after; then it is to be given a chance to see the world. Live in love so that he can become that which God created him to be. No child is a mistake!

A father is an epitome of strength and anchorage in the life of his child more so a teenager. He is the first provider of Education(both formal and informal) to the life of his children. This education remains the key to the doors of a successful life this child awaits in the future.

It isn't easy in this modern culture to cultivate friendship because generally life has become too busy for such activities. But a father's attitude and language towards his children must at all times be friendly and soulful. He should be a true friend at all seasons and time. A correct peaceful ambiance isn't necessarily needed for a child to get close to his dad for any questions or advice.

In the Voice of a father; the difference between bad and good is known by his children. In his voice; a child learns to respect the old and the young. Through a father's voice; a prediction of a bright future is brought close to reality to the life of his children. From a father's voice; I am certain a child's progeny has a leader, provider and protector because a father's voice anchors authority and wires it in the system of his children.

In the simplest way possible, I encourage each one of you out there, to realize that, children are not a mistake, God had a special purpose why he used us as vessels to bring them to the world.

I think this problem is too big to be viewed in a personal context. Our society has really witnessed a change in our older views of gender and their respective roles.

In the times of our fathers and mothers, women had no say in the society. Leadership was left for man who later became dominant and his figure remained a very powerful source of wisdom, leadership and growth to our then children. This also empowered our male children because as they grew, they knew that their family legacy will one day depend on them. They were taught how to be strong and appreciate their supernatural roles: to lead the way. Sons were taught on the values of appreciating being masculine plus the responsibility it came with. They hence grew stronger and it transcended from generation to generation.

But as we advanced in Education, our views and scope started to change slowly. We started witnessing strong African women like Miriam Makeba, Wangare Maathai; fighting so hard to empower women and the girl child in the society. The late Margaret Ogola in her work The River and source writes, " a home without a daughter is like a river without a source." The efforts of these great women plus others formed a strong foundation for the strong African woman that we see today.

Back to my point, the empowerment of women and the girl child continued until we forgot about the boy child. We shifted our attention more on the girl child and literally neglected our boy child. Slowly again because it is the same boy of today who becomes the father of tomorrow, we find out that our fathers have also been forgotten in the society. Most of our children will prefer a mother to a father when it comes to asking questions or counselling. Fathers are only needed when it comes to providing needs in the family.

Our mothers have also made these people look bad in our eyes as children. Small fights and misunderstanding between our parents is brought to us children. Of course we will tend to side with mothers like I did and we end up judging our fathers harshly. I use this book to encourage me and all who feel the same way to go back home. Because our men are weak today. We are born in weak homes, brought up by a weak parenting thus a weaker product of men. My good friend Loise Mwangi refers to them as 'boys'. These are men who have ran away from their key roles at home to being tomato and onion providers; women on the other hand are the ones paying bills etcetera. This wasn't God's plan! No!

The Voice of a father must be brought back and be inculcated to the growth of our children. A father is a very important figure when it comes to the development of a girl child too. He is the first person who is supposed to tell the daughter the dangers of making wrong choices concerning friends more so the male friends. This is because a father knows the behaviour and the, ' go get her' mentality of the young growing boys. He knows that these boys are only there to taste the waters and create experience from a young teenage girl. When proper friendship is nurtured between a father and a daughter, more than anything, we can be sure that we have secured and saved a generation.

A father is also a symbol of authority in the lives of a child more so a male child. He acts as the first role model for his growth. He shapes his thinking and the whole aspect of his life. A father brings the old flavour and ways of life to the attention of his son. By so doing, this boy grows up on a solid unshakeable grounds of wisdom and understanding.

Readers, my main aim here is not to make us forget our mothers or a girl child again, but let us in an inclusive way try to nurture and empower all our children regardless of their gender. But most importantly, I pray that my generation can try and save the endangered extinction male species in our society, by bringing back that long forgotten voice of a father in the family.

 All those factors that once protected our social structure have worn out. Our villages turned to small towns. Our parents have been subjected to money hunting schemes. They are too busy making other people's businesses thrive in the name of careers while their home businesses being swamped. The today child is left to research and get answers for himself.

The children have been empowered and too much freedom given to them. Education has become a tool for judgment other than change.

I am writing this book when as a country we are facing challenges in the education sector.

Who is to blame? Should we blame teachers? What can teachers do? Let me talk about this because I have an upper hand with a background in teaching. I know it is unethical for corporal punishment to take place in schools. Caning at times doesn't necessarily mean that the students will be morally upright. What ought to be observed is one simple thing; identifying the problem and having the correct weapon for it.

A teacher plays a very important role in the upbringing of a child. Children spend 70 percent of their lives in a teacher's hands. Knowing this should strike teachers to know the sharp, shaping influence they have over these kids. What should be done? What should teachers do? Teachers must at all time try to go beyond classroom when it comes to dealing with students. Try and interact with these kids, inculcate in them values of prayers, faith in who they are and what God expects from them, pray with them, motivate them to follow their dreams, maybe Jairo was poor in English but good in sports, it is the responsibility of a keen teacher to identify this and help Jairo maximize his potential in sports. This will make Jairo feel that he also has a special space in school, thus he will enjoy his time in in school. Do you think Jairo can have discipline issues if he is enjoying what he is doing? I guess no. Prayer plus actions.

Parents have a role to play too. Charity begins at home. Payment of school fees and sending your children to boarding schools with a notion that teachers will take charge is what fuels the whole issues of bad behavior among our children both at school and home.

You must spare time for your children. Help teachers in praying and moulding your children. I don't want to sound like I am blind to the fact that we are developing and things are changing, but facts be told, we are heading nowhere if we are blind to where we are coming from. This young people are the fathers and mothers of our grandchildren. Our future depends on what we feed them today. Solomon reminds us again in proverbs 29:17. Discipline your son and he will give rest and delight to your heart. "As a parent you are the role model and the first teacher to your children.

Many of our children have been raised by single parents. Mostly by their mothers. The male voice in the family is so important to the growth of a child. The Bible States that the words of a father must be heard and respected. The God Lord speaks to the two: father and son, for he has a supernatural plan and wish for them. " And He shall turn the heart of the fathers to the children, and the heart of the children to their fathers, lest I come and smite the earth with a curse. (Mal 4:6). We, the fathers, are, according to me, and I stand to be corrected, we are the reason why our society is failing. The heaven is punishing our generation for our mistakes. Our children are being punished for our mistakes.

Family breakups, fights and the image we give our children reflects on their characters. These are children who will also divorce their respective spouses. These are the children who will beat their wives. They are the people who will be bar fly. Why? Because of what we feed them as they grow.

The church has also a role to play in molding these children. Our church today has turned to be entertainment zones. Our men of God being the Champions and leaders of these entertainments. Our places of worship have turned to places of warship like I said earlier. Just recently, an apostle was caught stealing bear from a bar. Another one caught eating one of his 'sheep' in church. Before we could come to terms with that, another one was caught selling church seats. It has grown worse to the extent that others were caught on camera beating up old granny in church.

With the advent of a viral social media plus the liberty our children have today, all these things are gotten by them. If the Shepherd is a sleep, imagine what happens to the flocks he is looking after. The then values that were upheld because of a strong church we had have been eroded. Our rot exposed and this is evident in what is going on in our schools.

We have divided ourselves from our social backgrounds. We have no foundation. Parenting has become a guess work. We are not praying. Men of God, a line has been drawn, you will be judged harshly. Do not allow the devil take over the world while you know your mandate. Stand tall with the word of God. Go everywhere, in every corner of this world, preach about our one true God. Fight this battle head on because divinity is with you and for you.

Our media has a hand in this too. The content they show us has greatly influenced our children. This is what Doctor Timothy Gatara will refer to as, 'the poverty of the mind.' We have forgotten to use our media to enhance and promote our culture plus our social beliefs and practices, to promote the word of God, instead used this platform to promote the already structured, accepted and known white culture. Our African child has been forced to learn from a culture he isn't able to relate to. They are dancing to music they don't know. Our children have been exposed to the use of guns while we hide a jembe from their eyes. We have exposed them to pornography , and when they practice what they have learned, quick we are to judge them.

Divide this society from our core Christian values and beliefs and you will not fail to witness what is going on. Unless we understand where we are coming from, we will not know where we are heading to.

This is a struggle that can not be won if we are divided minded. It takes a village to raise a child. Let us not continue to fuel our already burning society by being blind to logic, and reality. Let us face the devil all of us through prayers and fasting.

Our media can embrace truth and promote our Christian values and practices if we choose to do something. Teachers can become parents, motivators and installers of curriculum and hope to students if we choose to do something. Our husbands and wives can come back to their senses and go back to bring honor and dignity in matrimony if we choose to do something. Our children can become whole again and focus on taking responsibility to building their world using their creative minds and energy if we choose to do something. Our men of God can go back to being our spiritual guidance and parents if we choose to do something.

And the only thing to do is by going back to the basics. By men going back to their knees. The devil is the enemy and prayer is the weapon. And men are stronger if they are the once to lead in this fight.

"Love is the most overused word in the English language." So it is said. I agree.

To grow in love in a world defined by power, money, and influence is a hard task. Modern conveniences such as electronic equipment, gadgets, and tools as well as entertainment through television, magazines, and the web have predisposed us to confine our attention mostly to physical needs and wants. As a result, our concepts of self-worth and self-meaning are muddled. To be honest, this has been the greatest challenge most people go through. We all have failed time without number to strike a balance between the material thing and the soulful world. Love has been put in the middle of this and I regret to admit that, human beings on several occasions have found themselves trying to use one to get the other. Well, this justifies the many heartbreaks experienced daily among couples.

First, to grow in love entails looking inside; searching for meaning, recognition of ones potentials and pursuing ones purpose on earth.

Introspection or looking inside goes beyond recalling the things that happened in a day, week, or month.

You need to look closely and reflect on your thoughts, feelings, beliefs, and motivations. Periodically examining your experiences, the decisions you make, the relationships you have, and the things you engage in, which provides useful insights on your life goals, on the good traits you must sustain and the bad traits you have to discard if you are interested in finding a long-term relationship. Moreover, it gives you clues on how to act, react, and conduct yourself in the midst of any situation. Like any skill, introspection can be learned; all it takes is the courage and willingness to seek the truths that lie within you. The greatest form of romance comes after one knows how to love themselves first. This can only be achieved if you have knowledge about yourself. Why do you think you want to know other people while you have no clue of who or what you are?

To grow in love is to pause first and try to develop your own potentials.

Religion and science have differing views on matters of the human spirit. Religion views people as spiritual beings temporarily living on Earth, while science views the spirit as just one dimension of an individual. Mastery of the self is a recurring theme in both Christian (Western) and Islamic (Eastern) teachings. The needs of the body are recognized but placed under the needs of the spirit. Beliefs, values, morality, rules, experiences, and good works provide the blueprint to ensure the growth of the spiritual being. In Psychology, realizing ones full potential is to self-actualize. In my psychology class, Maslow identified several human needs: physiological, security, belongingness, esteem, cognitive, aesthetic, self-actualization, and self transcendence. James, earlier categorized these needs into three: material, emotional, and spiritual. When you have satisfied the basic physiological and emotional needs, spiritual or existential needs come next. Achieving each need leads to the total development of the individual. Perhaps the difference between these two religions and psychology is the end of self-development: Christianity and Islam see that self-development is a means toward serving God, while psychology view that self-development is an end by itself.

Regardless of both takes, what matters is that, development of your own skills and potential makes you a free bird to fly in any direction. It gives you confidence to face your world. Love becomes stronger if you know you have your dreams and visions accomplished. It gives one peace, the correct breeding grounds for love.

To grow in love is to search for meaning.

Religions that believe in the existence of God such as Christians, Judaism, and Islam suppose that the purpose of the human life is to serve the Creator of all things. Several theories in psychology propose that we ultimately give meaning to our lives. Whether we believe that life's meaning is pre-determined or self-directed, to grow in love also is to realize that we do not merely exist. We do not know the meaning of our lives at birth; but we gain knowledge and wisdom from our interactions with people and from our actions and reactions to the situations we are in. As we discover this meaning, there are certain beliefs and values that we reject and affirm. Our lives have purpose.

A good woman will make a good man realize his purpose on earth. This purpose puts all our physical, emotional, and intellectual potentials into use; sustains us during trying times; and gives us something to look forward to-a goal to achieve, a destination to reach. A person without purpose or meaning is like a drifting ship at sea. With a good woman, I am more than certain that you have a great friend, epitome of strength behind you propelling you to your success or towards fulfilling your purpose on earth. A man without purpose isn't fit to live.

To grow in love means: honor first: to be honored!

We have all heard these classic sayings before: what goes around comes around, what you see is what you get and you get what you give.

Sure, these sayings get preached over and over again with creative different wordings and twists to the point that they have become cliché and even tiring for us to hear. I agree! However, there is a reason why these get preached over and over again and that is because most of us need constant reminders, and well, some of us just can't bring ourselves to truly apply these wise teachings into our lives. What a shame!

We want to get it right and achieve successful love. Really we do- but our emotions and mind games always mess with us from doing what we already know deep down is right. Not to mention our pride, which is the greatest enemy when it comes to our dating and love lives. So here is the infamous saying one more time for you to read, digest and remember the next time you feel frustrated and catch yourself scratching your head as to why you are not having the relationship success you want: You Get What You Give. Really, it's true.

Often, we focus on what we are getting or not getting in a relationship and never really bother to back track and see what we may have done to receive what we are getting. Sure, there are times when life is just unfair and we get taken for granted and advantage of, but for the most part, we are having the type of relationship we have created with someone else and brought upon ourselves. Even in the cases in which we are being taken for granted, it is also because we are doing something to bring that on. If someone is taking you for granted or using you, for example, it is because you are presenting yourself in such a way that makes people feel like they can treat you that way.

It may sound cold and mean, but we do receive majority of bad behavior from our partners simply because we have given them permission to. Face it, if you truly would not accept being taken for granted, they would never have the chance to do it and hurt you because you just would not be around to allow them to do so. In other words, we are, most of the time, in control of how we are treated by others in the dating world (and in other fields of our lives).

Hell isn't made for sinners and if it is, then the biggest part in hell belongs to a man who will receive bread from his woman and give her stones in return. A good man is a blessing in the life of a good woman. She enjoys her life on earth. Her beauty is sparked more to shine and brighten his life. She becomes a subject of discussion on the lips of men and women of the world. She is accepted on Earth because she is able to live right. And anything that is accepted on earth is accepted in heaven -so does the good book say.

If you treat people you date kindly, with respect and consideration to their feelings, chances are that you will get the exact treatment from them. However, if you are really good to someone and they give you nothing in return but you continue to stick around, just remember that you have given them the message and a green light to go ahead and treat you negatively and they can still count on you to stay.

So remember this is not just what you give to others in order to get what you want in return, but also about what you give to yourself: and it is crowned by honoring your mate! When you honor them, you'll receive it too, maybe not from them, but from God! I appreciate you for taking your time to read the first part of this work. We've been tackling the roles of man to his family, friends and God. In the next part, I motivate us. Using my personal experience, work, vision and mission plus how it worked for me. Remember, if it did work for me, why not you? I call it: Turning Point! God bless you.

<u>Carry On.</u>

It will be will be wrong if I finish this book without motivating you and just encouraging you to keep on carrying on.

To single mothers or fathers out there. To orphans or to the childless. To drunkards or the lost in; substance abuse, lust, gambling. To the jobless. This one is for you. I will be very brief and straightforward to help us grasp the little knowledge that we can to help us in tackling these challenges and many more that we face.

Friends, many are we who have been to situations where we have been disqualified by society even before presenting our resumes or credentials or before showing what you can. Some will judge you harshly for your past mistakes. Men will reject you because you have a tummy or you have a child or a sickness that sends them away for fear of responsibilities. Women will reject you because you are swimming in abject poverty or you are a drunkard and every coin that you get finds its way to the hands of the brewer. Employers will reject you because you have no good papers or academic experience or qualifications. All these and many more are some of the impossible situations we go through day by day. If you are in such situations above, here is your word: Apostles Paul, one of the greatest (if not the greatest) writers of the New testament, had a glitch (imperfection) in speech. Paul wasn't that eloquent as many would have thought. It is because of this weakness that he goes in the pages of history as one of the greatest writers and thinker as far as theology is concerned. His glitch became his gift. His disqualification became his qualification.(Read 2 Corinthias 10:8-13). Listen, how many books did Martin Luther King write? How about Barack Obama? How about PLO Lumumba? 1,2 or none, but why? These are just some of the greatest orators the world has or ever had. Because they were gifted with speech;

Instead of writing, they spoke out there hearts to the people!

Joseph was rejected by his family, Moses had speech problems, Samson was lustful, Abraham was old, the list is endless, David was young, but through all these people, great works of God came to life. Friends, it's possible. Stand and make a step of faith today. Go ahead and fulfill that which God placed in you.... It doesn't matter if you are an orphan, childless, husbandless, jobless or clueless! God created you for a purpose! Yes you can help change this world in your own capacity the way you are. It doesn't matter how bad I was yesterday. Today I encourage you to know that, sharks were born swimming, you and I learnt how to walk through pain and fall. We are not perfect. We all have our own glitches, but inside the imperfections lay our gifts.

Everyone at some point of his or her life, has dreamt of being somebody special, somebody big. Who hasn't fantasized about being the one who hits the game-winning homer? Who hasn't dreamed of being the homecoming queen? And how many times have we dreamt of being rich, or successful, or happy with our relationships?

Often, we dream big dreams and have great aspirations. Unfortunately, our dreams remain just that, dreams. And our aspirations easily collect dust in our attic.

This is a sad turn of events in our life. Instead of experiencing exciting adventures in self actualization, we get caught up in the humdrum of living from day-to-day just barely existing.

But you know what? Life could be so much better, if only we learnt to aim higher. John Mason in his book, (The impossible is Possible), pens and I agree, "a man with no dreams isn't worth living." In other words, vision drives you, gives your life meaning, you get motivated to keep on waking up every morning. That's the power of dreaming.

The most common problem to setting goals is the word impossible. Most people get hung up thinking I can't do this. It's too hard. It's too impossible. No one can do this.

One of my bosses; Mrs. Mbocha loved me so much. Not because of any charm I used on her, but because of the Spirit of, ' I can do it', that she saw in me the first time I went to seek for a teaching job in the school I have come to love over the past few years: Great Vision Girls High school. I went to apply for that job and in my portfolio I had nothing like a degree certificate . I had just dropped out of college due to school fees challenges. She believed in me and gave me a class to teach. I grabbed the opportunity and gave my best in any class I attended. Through hard work, research and honoring the chance I had at my disposal, I earned respect, love and acceptance in this field. I worked for four years and I felt great knowing that, the belief and courage I took towards getting the job despite the fact that I had no degree really defines who I am today. It is therefore possible my dear readers.

However, if everyone thought that, there would be no inventions, no innovations, and no breakthroughs in human accomplishment, then you can imagine where we can be as a generation. All this massive ideas and innovation we see and enjoy today is because, someone somewhere believed that it is possible.

Remember that scientists were baffled when they took a look at the humble bumblebee. Theoretically, they said, it was impossible for the bumblebee to fly. Unfortunately for the bumblebee no one had told it so. So fly it does.

On the other hand, some people suffer from dreaming totally outrageous dreams and not acting on them. The result? Broken dreams, and tattered aspirations.

If you limit yourself with self-doubt, and self-limiting assumptions, you will never be able to break past what you deem impossible. If you reach too far out into the sky without working towards your goal, you will find yourself clinging on to the impossible dream.

Try this exercise. Take a piece of paper and write down some goals in your life. Under one header, list down things that you know you can do. Under another header, write the things

That you might be able to do. And under one more, list the things that are impossible for you to do.

Now look at all the headers strive every day to accomplish the goals that are under things that you know you can do. Check them when you are able to accomplish them. As you slowly are able to check all of your goals under that heading, try accomplishing the goals under the other header-the one that reads, you might be able to do.

As of the items you wrote under things I could do are accomplished, you can move the goals that are under things that are impossible for you to do to the list of things that you might be able to do.

As you iterate through this process, you will find out that the goals you thought were impossible become easier to accomplish. And the impossible begin to seem possible after all.

You see, the technique here is not to limit your imagination. It is to aim high, and start working towards that goal little by little. However, it also is unwise to set a goal that is truly unrealistic.

Those who just dream towards a goal without working hard end up disappointed and disillusioned.

On the other hand, if you told someone a hundred years ago that it was possible for man to be on the moon, they would laugh at you. If you had told them that you could send mail from here to the other side of the world in a few seconds, they would say you were out of your mind. But, through sheer desire and perseverance, these impossible dreams are now realities.

Thomas Edison once said that genius is 1% inspiration and 99% perspiration. Nothing could be truer. For one to accomplish his or her dreams, there has to be had work and discipline. But take note that that 1% has to be a think-big dream, and not some easily accomplished one.

Ask any gym rat and he or she will tell you that there can be no gains unless you are put out of your comfort zone. Remember the saying, 'No pain, no gain?' That is as true as it can be.

So dream on, friend! Don't get caught up with your perceived limitations. Think big and work hard to attain those dreams. As you step up the ladder of progress, you will just find out that the impossible has just become a little bit more possible.

God bless you all. Thanks a lot for your patience and dedication to reading this work page to page. Kindly put this into practice and may the almighty God open doors for you and your family in Jesus name.

42

Table of Contents

Printed by Books on Demand GmbH, Norderstedt / Germany